I WAS BORN TO BE A SISTER

I Was Born

to Be a
Sister

By Akaela S. Michels-Gualtieri

Illustrated by Marcy Dunn Ramsey

Platypus Media, LLC
Washington DC USA
2001

Akaela S. Michels-Gualtieri
 I was born to be a sister / by Akaela S. Michels-Gualtieri; illustrated by
Marcy Dunn Ramsey.
        p. cm.
Summary: A girl who felt born to be a sister wants to send her baby
brother back after he screams during her birthday party, knocks down her
cheese tower, and other baby behavior.
 ISBN 1-930775-03-2 (alk. paper)
 [1. Babies—Fiction. 2. Sisters—Fiction. 3. Brothers and
sisters—Fiction. 4. Sibling rivalry—Fiction.] I. Ramsey, Marcy Dunn,
ill. II. Title.
 PZ7.M5817 Iae 2001
 [E]—dc21
                                                    2001000615

Watch for the other books in this series:
I Was Born to be a Brother
I Was Born to be a Mother
I Was Born to be a Father

Published by Platypus Media LLC, 627 A Street NE, Washington, DC 20002, USA.

PlatypusMedia.com

ISBN 1-930775-03-2

10 9 8 7 6 5 4 3 2 1

Edited by Ellen E.M. Roberts, Where Books Begin, New York, NY
Designed by Douglas Wink, Inkway Graphics, Jersey City, NJ
Produced by Millicent Fairhurst, MF Book Production Services, New York, NY

Manufactured in the United States of America

To Mom and Dad—
who made me a sister!

Some girls were born
to be princesses.

Some were born
to be redheads.

I was born to be a sister.

When I was three, my baby brother was born. I was a sister at last. This was what I was meant to be!

In the beginning, it was so much fun.

I clapped my baby brother's feet together
to make him smile.

I sang "Rock-A-Bye-Baby" to him to make him fall asleep.

I squeezed a sponge
over his belly
to make him clean.

I taught him to slurp his
spaghetti at dinnertime.

But after a while, being a sister wasn't so fun anymore.

"Why do I have to be a sister?" I whispered to my mom.

"Can't we send him back?" I asked my dad when my brother wasn't listening.

My brother splashed water in my face when I was getting ready to do a somersault in the pool.

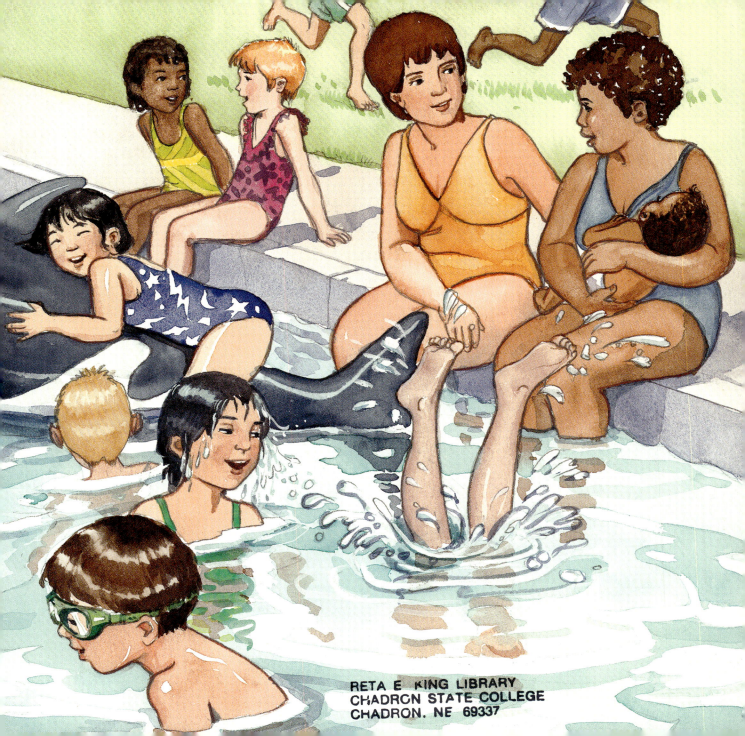

He crashed
into me
when
I was
doing
cartwheels.

He knocked over my cube tower
just when it was getting tall.

He screamed without stopping while everyone else sang "Happy Birthday" to me at my party.

By the time fall came, I hated being a sister.

"Maybe he can move into his own apartment,"
I told Mom.

"Maybe we'll lose him at the mall," I told Dad.

The best part of starting school was getting away from my baby brother. But when I came home, he was waiting for me.

He wanted to play castle. I showed him how to slay a dragon.

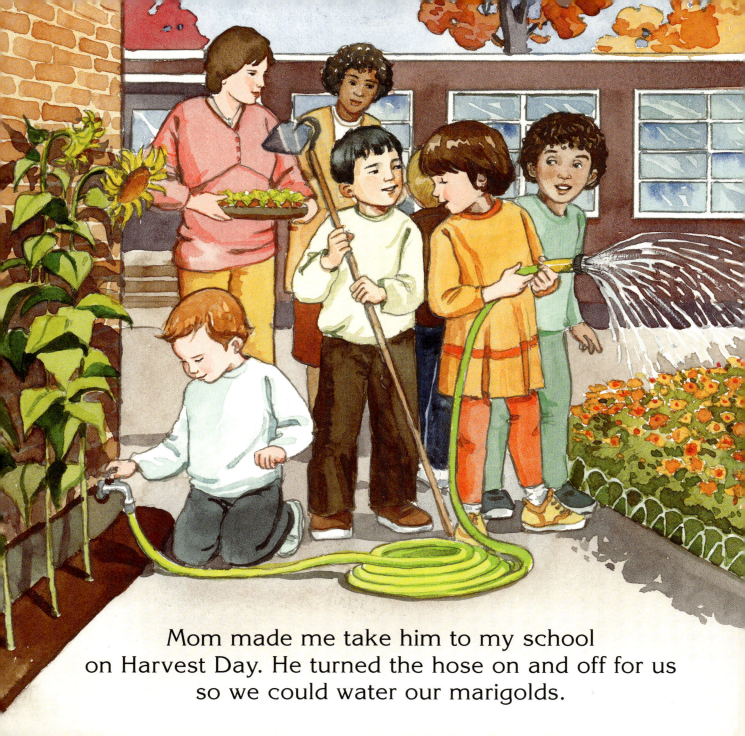

Mom made me take him to my school
on Harvest Day. He turned the hose on and off for us
so we could water our marigolds.

He brought all the red candies for me from Jack's birthday party.

Dad says he's learning to share.

Everywhere I go, he's always following me, asking questions and copying what I do. He remembers every word I say and every song I sing. It's a lot of work to be a sister.

It's a big job, but then,
I'm a big sister.